GREETINGS FROM
CHICAGO
ILLINOIS

GREETINGS FROM
CHICAGO
ILLINOIS

GREETINGS FROM
CHICAGO
ILLINOIS

GREETINGS FROM
CHICAGO
ILLINOIS

GREETINGS FROM
CHICAGO
ILLINOIS

GREETINGS FROM
CHICAGO
ILLINOIS

GREETINGS FROM
CHICAGO
ILLINOIS

GREETINGS FROM
CHICAGO
ILLINOIS

GREETINGS FROM
CHICAGO
ILLINOIS

GREETINGS FROM
CHICAGO
ILLINOIS

GREETINGS FROM
CHICAGO
ILLINOIS

GREETINGS FROM
CHICAGO
ILLINOIS

GREETINGS FROM
CHICAGO
ILLINOIS

GREETINGS FROM
CHICAGO
ILLINOIS

GREETINGS FROM
CHICAGO
ILLINOIS

GREETINGS FROM
CHICAGO
ILLINOIS

GREETINGS FROM
CHICAGO
ILLINOIS

GREETINGS FROM
CHICAGO
ILLINOIS

GREETINGS FROM
CHICAGO
ILLINOIS

GREETINGS FROM
CHICAGO
ILLINOIS

GREETINGS FROM
CHICAGO
ILLINOIS

GREETINGS FROM
CHICAGO
ILLINOIS

GREETINGS FROM
CHICAGO
ILLINOIS

GREETINGS FROM
CHICAGO
ILLINOIS

GREETINGS FROM
CHICAGO
ILLINOIS

GREETINGS FROM
CHICAGO
ILLINOIS

GREETINGS FROM
CHICAGO
ILLINOIS

GREETINGS FROM
CHICAGO
ILLINOIS

GREETINGS FROM
CHICAGO
ILLINOIS

GREETINGS FROM
CHICAGO
ILLINOIS

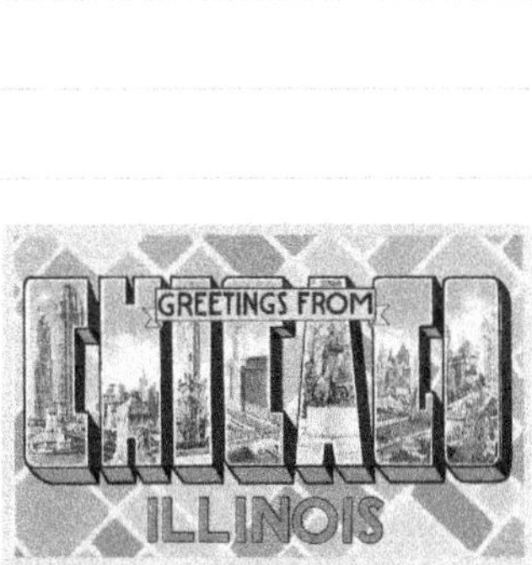
GREETINGS FROM
CHICAGO
ILLINOIS

GREETINGS FROM
CHICAGO
ILLINOIS

GREETINGS FROM
CHICAGO
ILLINOIS

GREETINGS FROM
CHICAGO
ILLINOIS

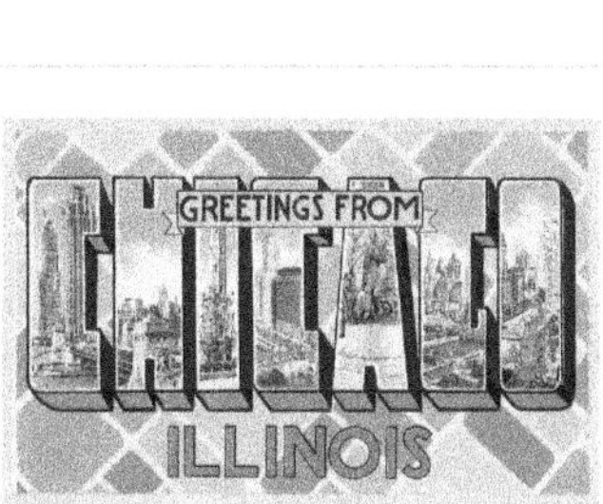
GREETINGS FROM
CHICAGO
ILLINOIS

GREETINGS FROM
CHICAGO
ILLINOIS

GREETINGS FROM
CHICAGO
ILLINOIS

GREETINGS FROM
CHICAGO
ILLINOIS

GREETINGS FROM
CHICAGO
ILLINOIS

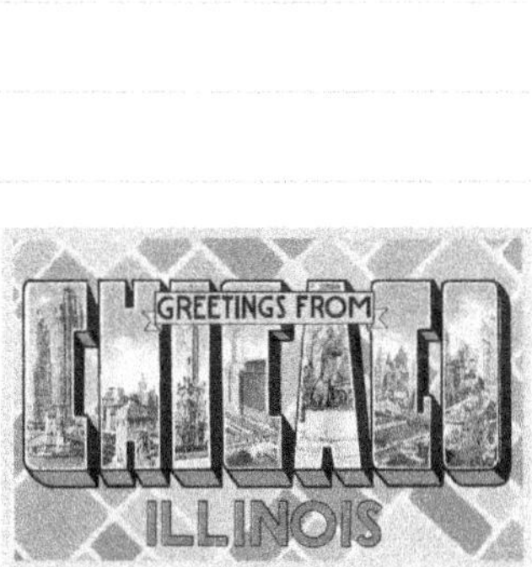
GREETINGS FROM
CHICAGO
ILLINOIS

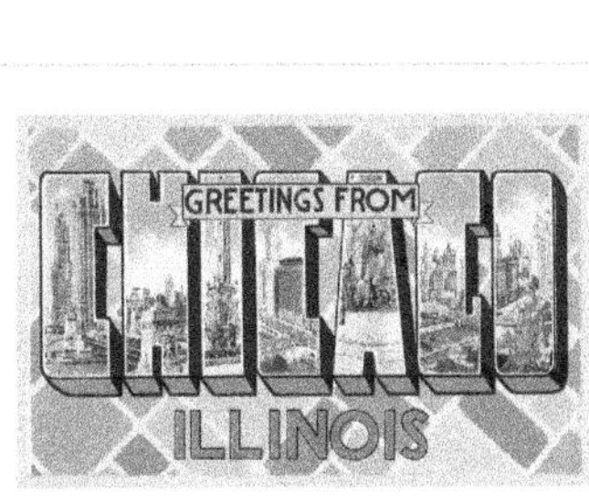
GREETINGS FROM
CHICAGO
ILLINOIS

GREETINGS FROM
CHICAGO
ILLINOIS

GREETINGS FROM
CHICAGO
ILLINOIS

GREETINGS FROM
CHICAGO
ILLINOIS

GREETINGS FROM
CHICAGO
ILLINOIS

GREETINGS FROM
CHICAGO
ILLINOIS

GREETINGS FROM
CHICAGO
ILLINOIS

GREETINGS FROM
CHICAGO
ILLINOIS

GREETINGS FROM
CHICAGO
ILLINOIS

GREETINGS FROM
CHICAGO
ILLINOIS

GREETINGS FROM
CHICAGO
ILLINOIS

GREETINGS FROM
CHICAGO
ILLINOIS

GREETINGS FROM
CHICAGO
ILLINOIS

GREETINGS FROM
CHICAGO
ILLINOIS

GREETINGS FROM
CHICAGO
ILLINOIS

GREETINGS FROM
CHICAGO
ILLINOIS

GREETINGS FROM
CHICAGO
ILLINOIS

GREETINGS FROM
CHICAGO
ILLINOIS

GREETINGS FROM
CHICAGO
ILLINOIS

GREETINGS FROM
CHICAGO
ILLINOIS

GREETINGS FROM
CHICAGO
ILLINOIS

GREETINGS FROM
CHICAGO
ILLINOIS

GREETINGS FROM
CHICAGO
ILLINOIS

GREETINGS FROM
CHICAGO
ILLINOIS

GREETINGS FROM
CHICAGO
ILLINOIS

GREETINGS FROM
CHICAGO
ILLINOIS

GREETINGS FROM
CHICAGO
ILLINOIS

GREETINGS FROM
CHICAGO
ILLINOIS

GREETINGS FROM
CHICAGO
ILLINOIS

GREETINGS FROM
CHICAGO
ILLINOIS

GREETINGS FROM
CHICAGO
ILLINOIS

GREETINGS FROM
CHICAGO
ILLINOIS

GREETINGS FROM
CHICAGO
ILLINOIS

GREETINGS FROM
CHICAGO
ILLINOIS

GREETINGS FROM
CHICAGO
ILLINOIS

Printed in the USA
CPSIA information can be obtained
at www.ICGtesting.com
CBHW020833260624
10675CB00006B/746

9 798385 404728